The Way of the Cross

The Traditional Devotion
newly presented by Andrew Moore

Kevin
Mayhew

First published in 1997 by
KEVIN MAYHEW LTD
Rattlesden
Bury St Edmunds
Suffolk IP30 0SZ

ISBN 1 84003 095 X
Catalogue No 1500153

0 1 2 3 4 5 6 7 8 9

Front cover illustration by Gabrielle Stoddart
Cover design by Jaquetta Sergeant
Typesetting by Louise Hill
Printed in Great Britain

Preface

The Way of the Cross is a long-established devotional practice. It has inspired artists, sculptors, poets and musicians to produce works of profound sensitivity. Each generation has to understand the Cross for itself, to open itself to the fundamental contradiction that lies at the heart of the Christian Faith.

This volume is offered as a resource to those who wish to follow the Way of the Cross, for those whose task it is to lead devotion, for those who may wish to make this journey alone in church, on the road, or at home. Alongside the traditional formulas, this selection brings together readings from Scripture and prayers from the Liturgy of the Church, together with some new material.

For each Station there is provided the traditional responses, two Scripture readings, a meditation and a choice of two prayers. The Appendix contains a selection of appropriate hymns and antiphons.

ANDREW MOORE

Acknowledgements

The texts of the opening prayers from *The Roman Missal* © 1973, International Committee on English in the Liturgy, Inc. All rights reserved. Adapted and used with permission.

Bible quotations are taken from *The New Jerusalem Bible* published and © Copyright 1985 by Darton Longman & Todd Ltd and Doubleday & Co Inc. and used by permission of the publisher.

Psalm texts © The Grail (England) from *The Psalms: A New Translation*, by permission of A. P. Watt Ltd.

THE WAY
OF THE CROSS

The Way of the Cross

THE JOURNEY BEGINS

The early Christians called themselves followers of the Way, because Jesus had said of himself, 'I am the Way, the Truth and the Life; no one can come to the Father except through me' (John 14:6). In following the Way of the Cross, we give particular and poignant expression to our Christian identity as followers of the Way. With prayer and meditation, we walk with Jesus into a deeper understanding of the mystery of our redemption. In contemplation of his suffering and death, we come to appreciate more fully the words of St John: 'God loved the world so much that he gave his only Son, so that everyone who believes in him may not be lost but may have everlasting life.' (John 3:16)

Scripture readings

Christ Jesus, being in the form of God, did not count equality with God something to be grasped. But he emptied himself, taking the form of a slave, becoming as human beings are; and being in every way like a human being, he was humbler yet, even to accepting death, death on a cross. And for this God raised him high, and gave him the name which is above all other names; so that all beings in the heavens, on earth and in the underworld, should bend the knee at the name of Jesus and that every tongue should acknowledge Jesus Christ as Lord, to the glory of God the Father.'

Philippians 2:6-11

or

The message of the Cross is folly for those who are on the way to ruin, but for those of us who are on the road to salvation it is the power of God.

1 Corinthians 1:18

Prayers

Lord God,
the Cross reveals the mystery of your love:
a stumbling block indeed for unbelief,
but the sign of your power and wisdom to us who believe.
Teach us so to contemplate your Son's glorious Passion
that we may always believe and glory in his Cross.
We make our prayer through Christ our Lord.
Amen.

Evening Prayer: Friday, Week II

or

Lord Jesus, our Saviour,
be our guide
as, unworthily, we follow in the steps of your Passion;
be our strength
in our sorrow for having offended you;
be our joy
in whatever sufferings and humiliations await us in this life,
that we may come to share eternal joy with you.
For you are Lord, for ever and ever.
Amen.

The First Station

Jesus Is Condemned to Death

℣   We adore you, O Christ, and we praise you.

℟   Because by your holy Cross you have redeemed the world.

Scripture readings

Pilate came outside and said, 'Look, I am going to bring him out to you to let you see that I find no case.' Jesus then came out wearing the crown of thorns and the purple robe. Pilate said, 'Here is the man.' When they saw him, the chief priests and the guards shouted, 'Crucify him! Crucify him!' Pilate said, 'Take him yourselves and crucify him: I find no case against him.' The Jews replied, 'We have a Law, and according to that Law he ought to be put to death, because he has claimed to be the Son of God.'

John 19:4-7

or

It is the God of Abraham, Isaac and Jacob, the God of our ancestors, who has glorified his servant Jesus whom you handed over and then disowned in the presence of Pilate after he had given his verdict to release him. It was you who accused the Holy and Upright One, you who demanded that a murderer should be released to you while you killed the Prince of Life.

Acts 3:13-15

Meditation

Jesus is condemned to death; who by? Was it by Pilate, the Pilate who could 'find no case against him'; Pilate the astute politician who, by allowing the crucifixion of the 'King of the Jews', was strengthening his own and Rome's control over an occupied and turbulent country?

Jesus is condemned to death; was it by the crowd, whipped up by mass emotion, egged on by those whose loathing of Jesus had turned to determined hatred?

Jesus is condemned to death; was it by us, by the condemnatory and rash judgements that we make, by our failure to insist on justice, by our indifference in the face of injustice?

Prayers

God of power and mercy,
who willed that Christ your Son
should suffer for the salvation of all the world,

grant that your people may strive
to offer themselves to you as a living sacrifice,
and may be filled with the fullness of your love.
We make our prayer through Christ our Lord.
Amen.

Evening Prayer: Friday, Week IV

or

Lord Jesus,
give us the strength to stand firm for what is right,
the wisdom to make such judgements
as we have to make
with fairness and integrity,
and the courage to suffer injustice
with dignity and compassion.
For you are Lord, for ever and ever.
Amen.

All   Our Father

Hail, Mary

Glory be to the Father

℣   Have mercy on us, O Lord.
℟   Have mercy on us.

All   I love you, Jesus, my love, above all things:
I repent with my whole heart for having offended you.
Never permit me to separate myself from you again.
Grant that I may love you always,
and then do with me what you will.

Hymn   Jesus, who condemns you?*
Who cries 'Crucify'?
Priest or politician?
Jesus, is it I?

or

At the cross her station keeping,
stood the mournful mother weeping,
close to Jesus to the last.

*See pages 40 and 41 for music.

The Second Station

Jesus Takes Up the Cross

℣   We adore you, O Christ, and we praise you.

℟   Because by your holy Cross you have redeemed the world.

Scripture readings

Yet ours were the sufferings he was bearing, ours the sorrows he was carrying, while we thought of him as someone being punished and struck with affliction by God; whereas he was being wounded for our rebellions, crushed because of our guilt; the punishment reconciling us fell on him, and we have been healed by his bruises. We had all gone astray like sheep, each taking his own way, and Yahweh brought the acts of rebellion of all of us to bear on him. Ill-treated and afflicted, he never opened his mouth, like a lamb led to the slaughter-house, like a sheep dumb before its shearers he never opened his mouth.

Isaiah 53:4-7

or

If anyone wants to be a follower of mine, let him renounce himself and take up his cross and follow me. Anyone who wants to save his life will lose it; but anyone who loses his life for my sake, and for the sake of the Gospel, will save it.'

Mark 8:34-35

Meditation

No one passes through life without any burden. Some burdens are given to us, some we carry on behalf of others, some we invent for ourselves; but the burden of the Cross is surely a weight too heavy for anyone to bear. They are 'too heavy for us, our offences', but the weight of the crosses we impose on others, the weight of the crosses given to us, the weight, the weight – all is taken up by Jesus.

Prayers

Lord God,
teach us the lessons of your Son's Passion,
and so enable us, your people,
to bear the yoke he makes light for us.
We make our prayer through Christ our Lord.
Amen.

Evening Prayer: Friday, Week I

or

Lord Jesus,
have mercy on us for we have sinned,
have mercy on us for adding to your burden,
have mercy on us for being your burden.
For you are Lord, for ever and ever.
Amen.

All   Our Father

Hail, Mary

Glory be to the Father

℣   Have mercy on us, O Lord.
℟   Have mercy on us.

All   I love you, Jesus, my love, above all things:
I repent with my whole heart for having offended you.
Never permit me to separate myself from you again.
Grant that I may love you always,
    and then do with me what you will.

Hymn   Heavy, oh too heavy,
weighs a world of hate;
Christ, be our redeemer,
Jesus, bear the weight.

or

Through her heart, his sorrow sharing,
all his bitter anguish bearing,
now at length the sword has passed.

The Third Station

Jesus Falls the First Time

℣   We adore you, O Christ, and we praise you.

℟   Because by your holy Cross you have redeemed the world.

Scripture readings 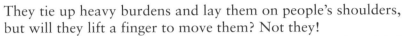 They tie up heavy burdens and lay them on people's shoulders, but will they lift a finger to move them? Not they!

Matthew 23:4

or

The girl on duty at the door said to Peter, 'Aren't you another of that man's disciples?' He answered, 'I am not.'

John 18:17

Meditation

The punishments already endured by Jesus – the imprisonment, the trial, the scourging, the crowning with thorns – would have been enough for anyone to endure. No wonder then that he should fall under the burden of the cross and the cruel tormenting of his torturers. How easily we fall, brought down by our blindness to see the obstacles in our way that can be avoided, our foolishness in putting obstacles in the way ourselves, but far worse if we should cause others to fall. *P 20 .*

Prayers

Lord Jesus Christ,
you were led to the Cross
to suffer the penalty of death
for the salvation of humankind:
in your mercy
grant us pardon for our past offences,
and by your power
preserve us from future falls.
Who live and reign for ever and ever.
Amen.

Midday Prayer: Friday, Week I

or

Lord Jesus,
when we fall, as sure we will,
have mercy on us;
when we fall, as sure we will,
give us strength and new hope;
when we fall, as sure we will,
forgive us and make us yours.
For you are Lord, for ever and ever.
Amen.

All   Our Father

Hail, Mary

Glory be to the Father

℣   Have mercy on us, O Lord.
℟   Have mercy on us.

All   I love you, Jesus, my love, above all things:
I repent with my whole heart for having offended you.
Never permit me to separate myself from you again.
Grant that I may love you always,
    and then do with me what you will.

Hymn   Perfect in obedience
to your Father's call,
Christ, creation's glory,
share creation's fall.

or

O, how sad and sore distressed
was that mother highly blest,
of the sole-begotten One.

The Fourth Station

Jesus Meets His Blessed Mother

℣ We adore you, O Christ, and we praise you.
℟ Because by your holy Cross you have redeemed the world.

Scripture readings

Yes, it was you who took me from the womb,
entrusted me to my mother's breast.
To you I was committed from my birth,
from my mother's womb you have been my God.
Do not leave me alone in my distress;
come close, there is none else to help me.

Psalm 21(22): 10-12

or

Now his mother and brothers arrived and, standing outside, sent in a message asking for him. A crowd was sitting round him at the time the message was passed to him. 'Look, your mother and brothers and sisters are outside asking for you.' He replied, 'Who are my mother and my brothers?' And looking round at those sitting in a circle round him, he said, 'Here are my mother and my brothers. Anyone who does the will of God, that person is my brother and sister and mother.'

Mark 3:31-35

Meditation

At Cana, Jesus had said to his mother, 'Woman, why turn to me? My hour has not come yet.' Now his hour has come and his mother is there for him, and with him. Mary did not always understand when her son was about his father's business and she may not, at this moment, have understood this heart-wrenching sight of her wounded and beaten son on his way to a certain and terrible death. But Mary's trust in God and her maternal love reached out beyond any lack of understanding and beyond the sorrow in her own heart, to be a support to her Son at the hour of his death.

Prayers

Lord Jesus Christ,
you chose the Virgin Mary to be your mother,
a worthy home in which to dwell.
By her prayers keep us from danger

and bring us to the joy of heaven.
Who live and reign for ever and ever.
Amen.

Common of the Blessed Virgin Mary

or

 Lord Jesus,
when our minds do not understand,
give us a trusting heart,
that we may come to understand
even as we will be understood.
For you are Lord, for ever and ever.
Amen.

All   Our Father

Hail, Mary

Glory be to the Father

℣   Have mercy on us, O Lord.
℟   Have mercy on us.

All   I love you, Jesus, my love, above all things:
I repent with my whole heart for having offended you.
Never permit me to separate myself from you again.
Grant that I may love you always,
and then do with me what you will.

Hymn   Where the humble suffer,
and the proud deride,
Mary, blessed Mother,
calls us to your side.

or

Christ above in torment hangs;
she beneath beholds the pangs
of her dying glorious Son.

The Fifth Station

SIMON OF CYRENE HELPS CARRY THE CROSS

℣   We adore you, O Christ, and we praise you.
℟   Because by your holy Cross you have redeemed the world.

Scripture readings   As they were leading him away they seized on a man, Simon from Cyrene, who was coming in from the country, and made him shoulder the cross and carry it behind Jesus.

Luke 23:26

or

Come to me, all you who labour and are overburdened, and I will give you rest. Shoulder my yoke and learn from me, for I am gentle and humble in heart, and you will find rest for your souls. Yes, my yoke is easy and my burden light.

Matthew 11:28-30

Meditation   Simon did not volunteer to help carry the cross; would we have volunteered? Yet, having helped in this unique and holy way, Simon's life and the lives of many others were changed, so that this imposed duty came to be seen as a wonderful and joyful privilege. None of us can take the place of Jesus; Simon did not take the cross from Jesus, but he did help. None of us can take everyone else's burdens but we can help and in helping we are changed.

Prayers   Lord God,
teach us the lessons of your Son's Passion,
and so enable us, your people,
to bear the yoke he makes light for us.
We make our prayer through Christ our Lord.
Amen.

Evening Prayer: Friday, Week I

or

Lord Jesus,
give us the sight
to see where help is needed,

the courage and generosity
to give the help that is needed
and the openness
to be changed by those whom we help.
For you are Lord, for ever and ever.
Amen.

All   Our Father

Hail, Mary

Glory be to the Father

℣   Have mercy on us, O Lord.
℟   Have mercy on us.

All   I love you, Jesus, my love, above all things:
I repent with my whole heart for having offended you.
Never permit me to separate myself from you again.
Grant that I may love you always,
and then do with me what you will.

Hymn   Christ, our only Saviour,
you must bear the loss;
yet give us compassion,
let us bear the cross.

or

Is there one who would not weep,
whelmed in miseries so deep,
Christ's dear mother to behold?

The Sixth Station

Veronica Wipes the Face of Jesus

℣   We adore you, O Christ, and we praise you.

℟   Because by your holy Cross you have redeemed the world.

Scripture readings   O Lord, hear my voice when I call;
have mercy and answer.
Of you my heart has spoken: 'Seek his face'.
It is your face, O Lord, that I seek;
hide not your face.

Psalm 26(27):7-8

or

Let your face shine on us and we shall be saved.

Psalm 79(80):4

or

'What can bring us happiness?' many say.
Lift up the light of your face on us, O Lord.

Psalm 4:7

Meditation   How often has a nurse wiped the fevered brow of a dying patient, not only bringing a welcome freshness and comfort but also an assurance of human compassion, love and companionship at a frighteningly lonely time? Veronica was privileged to wipe the actual face of Jesus; we are privileged to wipe the face of Jesus in caring for our brothers and sisters.

Prayers   Father,
open our hearts to the voice of your Word
and free us from the original darkness
that shadows our vision.
Restore our sight
that we may look upon your Son
who calls us to repentance and a change of heart,
for he lives and reigns with you for ever and ever.
Amen.

Collect for the Second Sunday of Lent

or

Lord Jesus,
give us the grace and graciousness
to serve you in all we meet,
especially those whose character, disfigurement
or suffering repels us.
For you are Lord, for ever and ever.
Amen.

All   Our Father

Hail, Mary

Glory be to the Father

℣   Have mercy on us, O Lord.
℟   Have mercy on us.

All   I love you, Jesus, my love, above all things:
I repent with my whole heart for having offended you.
Never permit me to separate myself from you again.
Grant that I may love you always,
and then do with me what you will.

Hymn   Christ, where now you suffer,
in each painful place,
let each act of kindness
still reveal your face.

or

Can the human heart refrain
from partaking in her pain,
in that mother's pain untold?

The Seventh Station

Jesus Falls the Second Time

℣   We adore you, O Christ, and we praise you.
℟   Because by your holy Cross you have redeemed the world.

Scripture readings   It happened that while he was travelling to Damascus and approaching the city, suddenly a light from heaven shone all round him. He fell to the ground, and then he heard a voice saying, 'Saul, Saul, why are you persecuting me?' 'Who are you, Lord?' he asked, and the answer came, 'I am Jesus, whom you are persecuting.'

Acts 9:3-5

or

As Simon Peter stood there warming himself, someone said to him, 'Aren't you another of his disciples?' He denied it saying, 'I am not.'

John 18:25

Meditation   The Cross is a contradiction, the weight of which bore down on Jesus' bruised shoulders and caused him to fall a second time. There are many contradictions that accompany us through life: we are called to holiness but are driven by weakness; we rejoice in, and yet despair of God's love. May we not despair of our strength to bear the stresses of life, because it is not our strength that will prevail but the Lord's.

Prayers   Lord Jesus Christ,
you were led to the Cross
to suffer the penalty of death
for the salvation of humankind:
in your mercy
grant us pardon for our past offences,
and by your power
preserve us from future falls.
Who live and reign for ever and ever.
Amen.

Midday Prayer: Friday, Week I

or

Lord Jesus,
when we fall, as sure we will,
have mercy on us;
when we fall, as sure we will,
give us strength and new hope;
when we fall, as sure we will,
forgive us and make us yours.
For you are Lord, for ever and ever.
Amen.

All   Our Father

Hail, Mary

Glory be to the Father

℣   Have mercy on us, O Lord.
℟   Have mercy on us.

All   I love you, Jesus, my love, above all things:
I repent with my whole heart for having offended you.
Never permit me to separate myself from you again.
Grant that I may love you always,
and then do with me what you will.

Hymn   Mortal flesh exhausted,
tortured sinews fail,
yet the spirit triumphs,
and the will prevails.

or

Bruised, derided, cursed, defiled,
she beheld her tender child,
all with bloody scourges rent.

The Eighth Station

The Women of Jerusalem Weep for the Lord

℣   We adore you, O Christ, and we praise you.

℟   Because by your holy Cross you have redeemed the world.

Scripture readings   Large numbers of people followed him, and women too, who mourned and lamented for him. But Jesus turned to them and said, 'Daughters of Jerusalem, do not weep for me; weep rather for yourselves and for your children.'

Luke 23:27-28

or

Blessed are those who mourn: they shall be comforted.

Matthew 5:5

Meditation

Many, like these women, had placed their hopes in Jesus. They had welcomed him as a king, they had seen him as one who would liberate them from oppression, they had seen him as the promise of freedom. The sight of him now – beaten, bloodied and weighed down by the very instrument of his impending death – drew profound tears. These were tears, not only for the apparent loss of their unfulfilled hopes, but tears of human sympathy and compassion for the pitiable and suffering figure who, even now, speaks out of concern for these women rather than for himself.

Prayers   God of power and mercy,
you destroy war and put down earthly pride.
Banish violence from our midst
and wipe away our tears,
that we may deserve to be called
your sons and daughters.
We make our prayer through Christ our Lord.
Amen.

Mass in time of war or civil disturbance

or

Lord Jesus,
help us to be ambitious for the higher gifts.
May we not revel in fantasies
of our own self-satisfying imagination
but come to the vision of your glory
in those who suffer or who are rejected by others
and ᵗ · themselves.
F   ᵣₑ Lord, for ever and ever. Amen.

℣
℟

All   I lo   ᵗngs:
I repe   ᵒffended you.
Never ₚ   ᵒu again.
Grant thaᵗ
and then do

Hymn   Still the faithful wₑ
stand beside the way,
weeping for the victimₛ
of the present day.

or

For the sins of his own nation,
saw him hang in desolation,
till his spirit forth he sent.

The Ninth Station

Jesus Falls the Third Time

℣   We adore you, O Christ, and we praise you.

℟   Because by your holy Cross you have redeemed the world.

Scripture readings

They came to a plot of land called Gethsemane, and Jesus said to his disciples, 'Stay here while I pray.' Then he took Peter and James and John with him. And he began to feel terror and anguish. And he said to them, 'My soul is sorrowful to the point of death. Wait here, and stay awake.' And going on a little further he threw himself on the ground and prayed that, if it were possible, this hour might pass him by. 'Abba, Father!' he said, 'For you everything is possible. Take this cup away from me. But let it be as you, not I, would have it.'

Mark 14:32-36

or

One of the high priest's servants, a relation of the man whose ear Peter had cut off, said, 'Didn't I see you in the garden with him?' Again Peter denied it; and at once a cock crowed.

John 18:26-27

Meditation

The Cross was a sign of great shame and great failure. The burden of expectation, laid upon him by those who had deserted him, weighed heavily on Jesus' body, racked with pain and exhaustion, and brought him down to fall a third time. Our own failures and our own sense of shame arise from vanity and misplaced pride. All too often we fall under the weight of vain and unrealistic expectations of our own abilities because we do not recognise the strength that the Lord provides.

Prayers

Lord Jesus Christ,
you were led to the Cross
to suffer the penalty of death
for the salvation of humankind:
in your mercy
grant us pardon for our past offences,
and by your power

preserve us from future falls.
Who live and reign for ever and ever.
Amen.

Midday Prayer: Friday, Week I

or

Lord Jesus,
when we fall, as sure we will,
have mercy on us;
when we fall, as sure we will,
give us strength and new hope;
when we fall, as sure we will,
forgive us and make us yours.
For you are Lord, for ever and ever.
Amen.

All　Our Father

Hail, Mary

Glory be to the Father

℣　Have mercy on us, O Lord.
℟　Have mercy on us.

All　I love you, Jesus, my love, above all things:
I repent with my whole heart for having offended you.
Never permit me to separate myself from you again.
Grant that I may love you always,
and then do with me what you will.

Hymn　Bowed beneath the burden
　of creation's pain,
Saviour, be beside us
when we fall again.

or

O thou mother! Fount of love!
Touch my spirit from above,
make my heart with thine accord.

The Tenth Station

Jesus Is Stripped of His Garments

℣   We adore you, O Christ, and we praise you.
℟   Because by your holy Cross you have redeemed the world.

Scripture readings

These people stare at me and gloat;
they divide my clothing among them.
They cast lots for my robe.

Psalm 21(22):18-19

or

The governor's soldiers took Jesus with them into the Praetorium and collected the whole cohort round him. And they stripped him and put a scarlet cloak round him, and having twisted some thorns into a crown they put this on his head and placed a reed in his right hand. To make fun of him they knelt to him saying, 'Hail, King of the Jews!' And they spat on him and took the reed and struck him on the head with it. And when they had finished making fun of him, they took off the cloak and dressed him in his own clothes and led him away to crucifixion.

Matthew 27: 27-31

Meditation

We weave so many garments of self-deception, and clothe ourselves with robes of false dignity. To be stripped of these would cause us great humiliation because they hide the greater humiliation of the naked truth about ourselves. Jesus is stripped, not of pretension or vainglory but of the garments that till now have hidden the extent of the painful bruising and cuts that he has already suffered. Stripped of any softness or comfort, his suffering is now exposed to the full and ruthless force of his tormentors and the heartless ridicule of those who jeer at him.

Prayers

Be mindful, Lord,
of this your family,
for whose sake our Lord Jesus Christ, when betrayed,
did not hesitate to yield himself into his enemies' hands,
and undergo the agony of the Cross:
he who lives and reigns for ever and ever.
Amen.

Liturgy of Good Friday

or

Lord Jesus,
you alone are our protection and comfort;
may we wear the clothing of our Christian faith
with dignity and courage.
For you are Lord, for ever and ever.
Amen.

All   Our Father

Hail, Mary

Glory be to the Father

℣   Have mercy on us, O Lord.
℟   · Have mercy on us.

All   I love you, Jesus, my love, above all things:
I repent with my whole heart for having offended you.
Never permit me to separate myself from you again.
Grant that I may love you always,
and then do with me what you will.

Hymn   Church of God, resplendent
in the robes of pow'r,
be the Saviour's body,
share his triumph hour!

or

Make me feel as thou hast felt;
make my soul to glow and melt
with the love of Christ my Lord.

The Eleventh Station

JESUS IS NAILED TO THE CROSS

℣   We adore you, O Christ, and we praise you.

℟   Because by your holy Cross you have redeemed the world.

Scripture readings

Many dogs have surrounded me,
a band of the wicked beset me.
They tear holes in my hands and my feet
and lay me in the dust of death.

Psalm 21(22):17

or

Christ suffered for you and left an example for you to follow in his steps. He had done nothing wrong, and had spoken no deceit. He was insulted and did not retaliate with insults; when he was suffering he made no threats but put his trust in the upright judge. He was bearing our sins in his own body on the cross, so that we might die to our sins and live for uprightness; through his bruises you have been healed.

1 Peter 2:21-24

Meditation

The hammer, a tool of the carpenter's workshop, is now used to inflict the cruellest of blows, to bind this sacred body to the cross of death. The hammer hits hard, but the hammer does not strike on its own; it is wielded by another human hand. Our hands can do so much good, or so much harm – the choice is ours.

Prayers

Lord Jesus Christ,
when the whole world was shrouded in darkness
you mounted the wood of the cross
as the innocent victim for our redemption;
give us always that light
which will bring us to eternal life.
Who live and reign for ever and ever.
Amen.

Midday Prayer: Friday

or

Lord Jesus,
many are the blows we suffer,
mostly small, some great.
Give us the physical and emotional strength
to endure them, with and for you,
and the moral strength to avoid
being the cause of suffering to others.
For you are Lord, for ever and ever.
Amen.

All   Our Father

Hail, Mary

Glory be to the Father

℣   Have mercy on us, O Lord.
℞   Have mercy on us.

All   I love you, Jesus, my love, above all things:
I repent with my whole heart for having offended you.
Never permit me to separate myself from you again.
Grant that I may love you always,
and then do with me what you will.

Hymn   All the pow'rs of evil
join to strike the nail,
patience and compassion
silently prevail.

or

Holy Mother, pierce me through,
in my heart each wound renew
of my Saviour crucified.

The Twelfth Station

JESUS DIES ON THE CROSS

℣   We adore you, O Christ, and we praise you.

℟   Because by your holy Cross you have redeemed the world.

Scripture readings   Jesus knew that everything had now been completed and, so that the scripture should be completely fulfilled, he said: 'I am thirsty.' A jar full of sour wine stood there; so, putting a sponge soaked in the wine on a hyssop stick, they held it up to his mouth. After Jesus had taken the wine he said, 'It is fulfilled'; and bowing his head he gave up his spirit.

John 19:28-30

or

When the sixth hour came there was darkness over the whole land until the ninth hour. And at the ninth hour Jesus cried out in a loud voice, 'Eloi, Eloi, lama sabachthani?' which means, 'My God, my God, why have you forsaken me?' When some of those who stood by heard this, they said, 'Listen, he is calling on Elijah.' Someone ran and soaked a sponge in vinegar and, putting it on a reed, gave it to him to drink saying, 'Wait! And see if Elijah will come to take him down.' But Jesus gave a loud cry and breathed his last. And the veil of the Sanctuary was torn in two from top to bottom. The centurion, who was standing in front of him, had seen how he had died, and he said, 'In truth this man was Son of God.'

Mark 15:33-39

Meditation   Death is a dark moment, none so dark as this one. The Son of God dies, the human breath of God expires. The brutal finality of death casts a long and sorrowful shadow. But the horrifyingly painful end of this particular life is a poignant and indelible sign to us that God's love is not finite. The love of God takes hold of any known or imagined limits, and goes beyond them, through any suffering, beyond and through even the final catastrophe that we call death. Death is a silent moment, none so silent as this one where we hear the 'silence of eternity, interpreted by love'.

Prayers   Father,
as your Son was raised on the cross
his mother Mary stood by him,

sharing his sufferings.
May your Church be united with Christ
in his suffering and death
and so come to share in his rising to new life
where he lives and reigns with you and the Holy Spirit,
one God, for ever and ever.
Amen.

Feast of Our Lady of Sorrows

or

Lord Jesus,
by your death you showed us
that death itself is understood,
and that we, in our frail mortality,
are understood.
Be with us when we come to face our own death,
that we may be with you
in the glory of everlasting life.
For you are Lord, for ever and ever.
Amen.

All   Our Father

Hail, Mary

Glory be to the Father

℣   Have mercy on us, O Lord.
℟   Have mercy on us.

All   I love you, Jesus, my love, above all things:
I repent with my whole heart for having offended you.
Never permit me to separate myself from you again.
Grant that I may love you always,
and then do with me what you will.

Hymn   Lonely and forsaken,
in this dying breath,
love alone can bear him
through the veil of death.

or

Let me share with thee his pain
who for all my sins was slain,
who for me in torments died.

The Thirteenth Station

Jesus Is Taken Down from the Cross

℣ We adore you, O Christ, and we praise you.
℟ Because by your holy Cross you have redeemed the world.

Scripture readings

Pilate, astonished that he should have died so soon, summoned the centurion and enquired if he had been dead for some time. Having been assured of this by the centurion, he granted the corpse to Joseph who bought a shroud . . . and took Jesus down from the cross.

Mark 15:44-46

or

Simeon said to Mary his mother, 'Look, he is destined for the fall and for the rise of many in Israel, destined to be a sign that is opposed – and a sword will pierce your soul too – so that the secret thoughts of many may be laid bare.'

Luke 2:34-35

Meditation

Mary had been the first to hold the body of the infant Jesus, a joy mingled now with deep sorrow as she holds the dead and lifeless, the torn and twisted body of her crucified son. Mary had trusted in the greatness of God at the awesome news of her son's conception. Now, as her soul resonates with the pain and grief of all who are bereaved, her trust is no less profound. Her trust in God inspires and supports us, even at the hour of our own death.

Prayers

God of power and mercy,
you have made death itself
the gateway to eternal life.
Look with love on those who have died today
and make them one with your Son
in his suffering and death,
that, sealed with the blood of Christ,
they may come before you free from sin.
We make this prayer through Christ our Lord.
Amen.

Mass for the dying – adapted

or

Lord Jesus,
may we who pray to and reverence your mother,
the Mother of God,
be assured of her protection throughout our lives,
especially in the face of grave sickness and death.
For you are Lord, for ever and ever.
Amen.

All   Our Father

Hail, Mary

Glory be to the Father

℣   Have mercy on us, O Lord.
℟   Have mercy on us.

All   I love you, Jesus, my love, above all things:
I repent with my whole heart for having offended you.
Never permit me to separate myself from you again.
Grant that I may love you always,
and then do with me what you will.

Hymn   Arms that cradled Jesus,
both at death and birth,
cradle all who suffer
in the pains of earth.

or

Let me mingle tears with thee,
mourning him who mourned for me,
all the days that I may live.

The Fourteenth Station

Jesus Is Laid in the Tomb

℣   We adore you, O Christ, and we praise you.
℟   Because by your holy Cross you have redeemed the world.

Scripture readings   After this, Joseph of Arimathea, who was a disciple of Jesus – though a secret one because he was afraid of the Jews – asked Pilate to let him remove the body of Jesus. Pilate gave permission, so they came and took it away. Nicodemus came as well – the same one who had first come to Jesus at night-time – and he brought a mixture of myrrh and aloes, weighing about a hundred pounds. They took the body of Jesus and bound it in linen cloths with the spices, following the Jewish burial custom. At the place where he had been crucified there was a garden, and in this garden a new tomb in which no one had yet been buried. Since it was the Jewish Day of Preparation and the tomb was nearby, they laid Jesus there.

John 19:38-42

or

For my soul is filled with evils;
my life is on the brink of the grave.
I am reckoned as one in the tomb:
I have reached the end of my strength,
like one alone among the dead;
like the slain lying in their graves;
like those you remember no more,
cut off, as they are, from your hand.
You have laid me in the depths of the tomb,
in places that are dark, in the depths.

Psalm 87(88):4-7

Meditation   The thoughts of those who reverently laid the stiff, pale and lifeless body in the tomb were likely thoughts of failure, for so it seemed. Perhaps they were not even thoughts at all, just tears of sorrow, for there was reason to cry. Perhaps they were not even tears, just the huge and breathless emptiness that comes with profound grief. The body was laid to rest with reverence and respectful care. Was there hope; was there expectation? Would we have had hope; would we have expected? Do we have hope; do we have expectation? We have followed the Way, the Way of the Cross; we have followed the Way, the Way of Truth; we have also followed the Way, the Way of Life.

Prayers Give us grace, almighty God,
so to unite ourselves in faith
with your only Son,
who underwent death
and lay buried in the tomb
that we may rise again
in newness of life with him,
who lives and reigns for ever and ever.
Amen.

Night Prayer: Friday

or

Lord Jesus,
you are the Way, the Truth and the Life;
no one can come to the Father except through you.
By your suffering and death
you showed us the way
to the glory of the resurrection.
May we come to share that glory
and live with you for ever.
For you are Lord, for ever and ever.
Amen.

All Our Father

Hail, Mary

Glory be to the Father

℣ Have mercy on us, O Lord.
℟ Have mercy on us.

All I love you, Jesus, my love, above all things:
I repent with my whole heart for having offended you.
Never permit me to separate myself from you again.
Grant that I may love you always,
and then do with me what you will.

Hymn Christ, who came with nothing
from your mother's womb,
rest in destitution,
in a borrowed tomb.

or

By the cross with thee to stay,
there with thee to weep and pray,
this I ask of thee to give.

Conclusion or Optional Fifteenth Station

THE RESURRECTION OF THE LORD

℣   We adore you, O Christ, and we praise you.
℟   Because by your holy Cross you have redeemed the world.

Scripture readings

After this perishable nature has put on imperishability, and this mortal nature has put on immortality, then will the words of scripture come true: 'Death is swallowed up in victory. Death, where is your victory? Death, where is your sting? The sting of death is sin, and the power of sin comes from the Law. Thank God, then, for giving us the victory through Jesus Christ our Lord.

1 Corinthians 15: 54-57

or

Jesus Christ is the faithful witness, the first-born from the dead, the highest of earthly kings. He loves us and has washed away our sins with his blood, and made us a Kingdom of Priests to serve his God and Father; to him, then, be glory and power for ever and ever. Amen. Look, he is coming on the clouds; everyone will see him, even those who pierced him, and all the races of the earth will mourn over him. Indeed this shall be so. Amen. 'I am the Alpha and the Omega,' says the Lord God, who is, who was, and who is to come, the Almighty.

Revelation 1:5-8

Meditation

The cross, a symbol of despair and failure, or a symbol of triumph and victory? Perhaps when we see a cross or crucifix we see both. Even in glory the wounds of the cross are not erased from the body of the Risen Lord; they stand as a witness, a witness to his suffering, a witness to our woundedness – but they are borne on a glorious body. This glory, the glory of the Resurrection gives us hope and reveals to us the mystery and triumph of the Cross.

Prayers

Lord,
send down your abundant blessing upon your people
who have devoutly recalled the death of your Son
in the sure hope of the Resurrection.
Grant them pardon; bring them comfort.

May their faith grow stronger
and their eternal salvation be assured.
We ask this through Christ our Lord.
Amen.

The Liturgy of Good Friday

or

Lord Jesus,
the power of your Resurrection,
which won for us the victory over sin and death,
makes the Cross a symbol of glory.
May we always rejoice in that glory.
For you are Lord, for ever and ever.
Amen.

All   Our Father

Hail, Mary

Glory be to the Father

℣   Have mercy on us, O Lord.
℟   Have mercy on us.

All   I love you, Jesus, my love, above all things:
I repent with my whole heart for having offended you.
Never permit me to separate myself from you again.
Grant that I may love you always,
and then do with me what you will.

Hymn   Broken but triumphant,
birthing gain from loss,
let us share your glory,
let us share your cross.

APPENDIX

The following hymns or antiphons may be sung between stations. They may all be found in *Hymns Old & New* (Kevin Mayhew). The first number refers to the 'New Century' edition (1994); the second number in bold refers to the 'Revised and Enlarged: With Supplement' edition (1989).

Jesus, who condemns you?	(See below)	
At the cross her station keeping (Stabat Mater) (See photocopiable pages following for text)	42	
At the name of Jesus (One verse may be sung after every second station)	43	50
God of mercy and compassion	149	180
Jesus, remember me	324	717

HOLY CROSS 65 65
First Station

Text: Michael Forster
Music: Andrew Moore

CASWALL 65 65
First Station

Je - sus, who con - demns you? Who cries 'Cru - ci - fy'?

Priest or po - li - ti - cian? Je - sus, is it I?

Text: Michael Forster
Music: Friedrich Filitz

See photocopiable pages following for full text.

Other suitable hymns:

Abide with me	5	4
All ye who seek a comfort sure	24	32
By the blood that flowed from thee	70	76
Glory be to Jesus	137	165
Lord Jesus Christ, you have come to us	247	326
Lord Jesus, think on me	248	327
My song is love unknown	277	363
O come and mourn with me awhile	289	383
O sacred head ill-used	320	427a
O sacred head sore wounded	321	427b
On a hill far away	329	413
Sing my tongue the glorious battle	368	484
The head that once was crowned with thorns	396	524
The royal banners forward go	409	545
There is a green hill far away	412	540
Were you there	449	598
When I survey the wondrous cross	454	610

Photocopiable pages

The following pages have been designed to be photocopied
at 84% on A4 paper, and folded to produce a four-page
leaflet for congregational use.

RESPONSES

℣   We adore you, O Christ, and we praise you.
℟   Because by your holy Cross you have redeemed the world.

℣   Have mercy on us, O Lord.
℟   Have mercy on us.

I love you, Jesus, my love, above all things:
I repent with my whole heart for having offended you.
Never permit me to separate myself from you again.
Grant that I may love you always,
and then do with me what you will.

HYMN

Jesus, who condemns you?   *or*   **At the cross her station keeping (Stabat Mater)**

First Station

Jesus, who condemns you?
Who cries 'Crucify'?
Priest or politician?
Jesus, is it I?

At the cross her station keeping,
stood the mournful mother weeping,
close to Jesus to the last.

Second Station

Heavy, oh too heavy,
weighs a world of hate;
Christ, be our redeemer,
Jesus, bear the weight.

Through her heart, his sorrow sharing,
all his bitter anguish bearing,
now at length the sword has passed.

Third Station

Perfect in obedience
to your Father's call,
Christ, creation's glory,
shares creation's fall.

O, how sad and sore distressed
was that mother highly blest,
of the sole-begotten One.

Fourth Station

Where the humble suffer,
and the proud deride,
Mary, blessed Mother,
calls us to your side.

Christ above in torment hangs;
she beneath beholds the pangs
of her dying glorious Son.

Fifth Station

Christ, our only Saviour,
you must bear the loss;
yet give us compassion,
let us bear the cross.

Is there one who would not weep,
whelmed in miseries so deep,
Christ's dear mother to behold?

Sixth Station

Christ, where now you suffer,
in each painful place,
let each act of kindness
still reveal your face.

Can the human heart refrain
from partaking in her pain,
in that mother's pain untold?

Seventh Station

Mortal flesh exhausted,
tortured sinews fail,
yet the spirit triumphs,
and the will prevails.

Bruised, derided, cursed, defiled,
she beheld her tender child,
all with bloody scourges rent.

Eighth Station

Still the faithful women
stand beside the way,
weeping for the victims
of the present day.

For the sins of his own nation,
saw him hang in desolation,
till his spirit forth he sent.

Ninth Station

Bowed beneath the burden
of creation's pain,
Saviour, be beside us
when we fall again.

O thou mother! Fount of love!
Touch my spirit from above,
make my heart with thine accord.

Tenth Station

Church of God, resplendent
in the robes of pow'r,
be the Saviour's body,
share his triumph hour!

Make me feel as thou hast felt;
make my soul to glow and melt
with the love of Christ my Lord.

Eleventh Station

All the pow'rs of evil
join to strike the nail;
patience and compassion
silently prevail.

Holy Mother, pierce me through,
in my heart each wound renew
of my Saviour crucified.

Twelfth Station

Lonely and forsaken,
in this dying breath,
love alone can bear him
through the veil of death.

Let me share with thee his pain
who for all my sins was slain,
who for me in torments died.

Thirteenth Station

Arms that cradled Jesus,
both at death and birth,
cradle all who suffer
in the pains of earth.

Let me mingle tears with thee,
mourning him who mourned for me,
all the days that I may live.

Fourteenth Station

Christ, who came with nothing
from your Mother's womb,
rest in destitution,
in a borrowed tomb.

By the cross with thee to stay,
there with thee to weep and pray,
this I ask of thee to give.

Fifteenth Station (optional)

Broken but triumphant,
birthing gain from loss,
let us share your glory,
let us share your cross.

Michael Forster

*Ascribed to Jacopone da Todi,
trans. Edward Caswall*

THE WAY OF THE CROSS